AMEN

To Barbara,
May God bless
you and keep you
safe.

Much Love,
Charlotte
Mae

AMEN

by

Charlotte Mae

ISBN: 0-75960-800-8

This book is printed on acid free paper.

1stBooks - rev. 12/19/00

This book of poetry is dedicated to

The one and only Living God. Thank you for your love.

And to his son Jesus Christ. Thank you for your life.

And to each and every heart that accepts him as their Savior.

A Friend

*A friend is someone to treasure the love and loyalty they give is
something that you cannot measure.*
*Their part of all the things that you are and they stand by you
when you're silly, stupid, and even acting quite bizarre.*

*A friend won't complain when you are in need, they are giving
in every way and never show any greed.*
*They stand by you come what may and forgive you for all the
ugly things that you might say.*
*A friend gives their heart without reservations and follows you
down to all of your destinations.*

*A friend to me is someone I can trust and keeping them in my
life is always a great big must.*
*I share my thoughts and all of my dreams; we play games very
often, but never on opposite teams.*
*I love my friends and I have been blessed with many they shine
in my eyes just like a brand-new penny.*

Charlotte Mae

A Mother Friend

A mother is a friend who stands by you to the bitter end.
She sees you for whom you are her beloved child her shining star.
When you find it hard to smile, she's the one who will go that extra mile.
A mother's soul is beauty she takes care of you out of love not out of duty.

A mother is a friend who is always true and when you are down she always knows what to do.
She lifts you up whenever you fall she helps you always; she is there as soon as you call.
Her smile is warm and can brighten up any day; she always makes you feel better in that wonderful mother way.

A mother friend is what you are to me; I love you so very much; you've let me be who I want to be.
You taught me to love and helped me to see, that love from the heart is love that is free.
I see you as a gift from the Father above, I swear you arrived on the great wings of a dove.

A Mother's Love

A mother's love is so very great it's something most of us do not appreciate. We take for granted all the care that is given and it is in our ungratefulness that selfishness is driven.
We let most days slip right on by without thanking our mothers and we didn't even try.

A mother's love is so very true, she never lets us down, and she makes each day seem brand new. She heals us when we are sick or hurt and she's the first one to pick us up out the dirt. Her smile is as warm as the sun and she always makes us feel like we are her special one.

A mother's love comes without any price, she's the only one you can count on to always be very nice. She helps you find hope when there wasn't a way and she will love you and care for you until her dying day.

3

Charlotte Mae

A New Day

As I close my eyes before I rest
I stop and think did I do my personal best
Did I treat each person with love and respect
Did I do his work today or did I show neglect
The Lord is my friend and from him I get much
He turns my life into gold with just a single touch
The Lord makes it easy for us to find our way
He gives us chance after chance with each new day

As the world spins and time passes by
The Lord creates life with just a blink of an eye
With oceans of blue and mountains of white
God's eagle and love seem to take to flight
He offers us peace when there seems like no way
He offers us hope with each and every new day

As life grows ever cruel and people don't seem to care
When you can't find a friend and you're filled with despair
Just look into the eyes of someone you know not
You will find God's way there and to him you mean a lot
Heaven can be yours and he will show you the way
He opens his heart to you each and every new day.

A Rose Never to Wilt

Flowers are a gift of great color and smell
I've arranged so many and I know them so well
But there is one that is truly in bloom
He is the brightest color in all of the room

Thrones will prick and often break the skin
Believing in Jesus the healing can begin
They thrust for water and need sunlight to live
Everlasting life is what he came here to give

A rose is many colors and is given for many reasons
It is a flower to be offered through all of the seasons
Give to him all of your pain and guilt
For he truly is a rose never to wilt.

A Soldier's Prayer

*My Lord up above they have taught me to hate
and not to love, in the field I will go and who I will kill I do
not know. A child is in danger and to him I am only a
stranger. Peace is not what is taught here; we are filled with
evil, rage and fear.*

*My mission is a sad one and I cannot go home until
it is done. I will take the life that you have given and out
of their homes these people will be driven. Their eyes weep
with pain and in the end there will be nothing at all to gain.
War can only bring on hurt and the children and their
families will be put into the dirt.*

*My Lord and God up above I know that there's
a heaven made of love. Please show me the way and help
me to learn how to pray. No more blood should be shed
no more dreams should be dead. Help my heart to finally
see that it is only through you that we can be free.*

A Special Light

There is a special light that shines on us all
It helps us in the darkness so that we don't fall
We use it when the sun has gone down and it's
warmth is ever glowing and shines off a crown.

This special light helps you see when you are blind
It opens your heart and teaches evil to become kind.
A light that is soft, but touch it you cannot
A light that is warm and won't burn you; never
is it hot.

A special light is what makes God's love light shine
You enter his world and it's a golden magical shrine.
He touches your soul and makes it glow like gold
In his world you'll always be young and never will
you grow old.

Charlotte Mae

All is Fair

When you compare your life to others you wonder if all is fair
They have so much more and your cupboard seems so bare
You wish for things that only money could buy
And your life is gone within a blink of an eye

Feel the air and touch the trees and know that love is there
God's love will protect you and follow you everywhere
He blesses you with family and friends to stand by your side
He never forgets his promise and in trouble he does not hide

With open arms he accepts you with all your sin and shame
He will be there in an instant just simply call out his name
His heart is so big and you must know that is where you will live
Unconditional love is what he will always give.

All Praise

All praise to the father up above
He has graced us with forgiveness and his love
A broken heart he never turns away
A lost soul has only but to pray.

Give to him your sadness and your fear
Your prayers of need always he will hear
The joy of his love is such a wonderful treasure
To be in his presence will be my greatest pleasure.

All praise to the father up above
He has graced us with forgiveness and his love
Someday my gracious father I will meet
I will worship and honor and know my soul is now complete.

All Who Know Him

All who know him know he is King
For eternal life is what he was sent here to bring
He walks with the Lion and Lamb on either side
Your shame and guilt from him you never need to hide
He will love you with all of your sin
Just open your heart and let him come on in
His hands are scared, but still they can reach out
He hears your prayers so speak soft you never need to shout.

All who know him know his love is real
Peace within your soul is what you will begin to feel
He will help you see your life has so much worth
Remember you became his child right from birth
He is the one true friend that never will leave
And when you are sad he too will grieve
He a waits for you in heaven with his Father by his side
He is the groom of forgiveness and you his needing bride.

As the Sun

As the sun set on another day
I folded my hands and began to pray
I thanked my God for my family
As I spoke to him I felt so free
I knew he was listening, but I heard no reply
I trusted him though and never asked why?

As the sun rose the very next day
I folded my hands and began to pray
I asked for patience with each of my deeds
I asked he fulfill all of my needs
I felt God with me as I started my task
"Why do you love me so," I just had to ask?

As the sun set on another day
I looked to the sky and I heard God say
These colors are a sign of my love for you
"I send gold and red and a very soft blue
I wait here for you my child in my Kingdom above
Where I watch over you with kindness and all of my love."

Being Yourself

He accepts you as you are, to him you are a shining star

Being yourself is quite a task, for him you needn't ever wear a mask.

Your smile is his light; to him it is always shining bright

Being yourself also can be fun; for to him you are a very special one.

Yes...he accepts us the way we are and when we are sad he is never far.

Being yourself is what you do best and he'll never leave you; for you are part of his quest.

Blame Him Not . . .

*Facing life and some of its pain can make the strong seem
weak
We tend to blame God for our misfortune whenever our future
looks bleak
The suffering that a loved one goes through can make ones
heart grow cold
But, blame him not for he did not choose to punish the sick the
weak or the old.*

*For a child to suffer from birth goes way beyond unfair
But the Kingdom they will enter one cannot compare
We are told to pray and trust God, yet we stop believing in his
word
But, blame him not for in our grief our prayers they still are
heard.*

*When the ground has turned cold and a broken heart no
longer can worship his name
When Satin is laughing with great delight and thinks that he
has won at his own game
Please search your soul and let God back in, for you loved one
is now with the King
But, blame him not the angels will cry for new hope and new
beginnings he will bring.*

13

Charlotte Mae

But You Loved Me

When times were hard and friends were few
I was so confused and did not know what to do
I looked to the bottle and thought I saw hope
I drank until I finally was at the end of my rope
Some saw me as a waste; I drank until I felt free
I thought no one cared, but you loved me.

When the bottle was empty and so was my soul
Making me whole again became your goal
Filling my heart with a love that was pure
And living a good life is what I would endure
Complete and whole is what I wanted to be
I thought no one cared, but you loved me.

Getting high was now in the past
And living for God became such a blast
I was alive and life had so much to give
I finally found a reason to live
As I sang your praises I finally did see
I thought no one cared, but you loved me.

Dear David

David was quite a wonder for a boy
He killed a giant with what seemed a little toy
He praised his God with prayer and songs that he would sing
Till soon God said "To the Jews you will be King."
He served his God and remained to him true
Until he met Bathsheba whose husband would meet his do.

In love they fell, but to God's displeasure
How far David would go no one could measure
He wanted his love and cared not about the cost
Sending her husband into War knowing his life soon would be lost
They now were free to marry for Bathsheba a child she did conceive
Not knowing that very soon their joy, they would now have to grieve.

In David's darkest moment was when he finally saw the light
He had to get back with his God and make his wrongs become right
He fell to his knees and cried tears filled with guilt
As he looked around the temple for his God that he had built
As God looked upon his servant he knew his lesson he had learned
So happiness was bestowed him for now it was truly earned.

15

Do Not Grieve

Do not grieve for me because I must part I am going to God's kingdom to be in his heart. He will bless me and treasure me and keep me in his love. He will give me the freedom to soar like the white winged dove.

Do not grieve for me for I did not die, my life is just beginning so, please, do not cry. God's gift of eternity is so very great; I can see him and Jesus waiting at the gate.

Do not grieve for me for I will live on. It is through God's special promise you'll know I'm not gone. I will see you in time and together we will be, I'll be waiting with God when it's your turn to be set free.

Amen

Dream Not

As the night did fall and moon began to rise
I fell deep into a sleep as soon as I closed my eyes.
I dreamed of a man who was loving and kind
In a dream world of my own he wasn't very hard to find.
His clothes were like rags and no money he had
He seemed to be quite poor, but never acted sad.

He talked of a land and his father up above
He told me all I needed was a heart filled with love.
I dreamed he healed the sick and the lame they did walk
His voice was calm and soothing as the people heard him talk.
He offered each New Hope he said his life would pave the way
As my dream began to unravel, I knew I'd see him again someday.

The next morning as the sun filled the sky
I knew my soul was saved and soon began to cry.
I felt his love all around me and my soul was complete
No longer with Satan's evil would I have to compete.
Dream not my child for I am real
Your soul in now God's for I was the seal.

17

Charlotte Mae

Ever Glowing Light

As an ever-glowing light rose in the sky I looked down a path and I saw a drifter passing by. He told me of a king who has come to save my soul I laughed and turned and thought his life must be very dull. People came running to see a baby boy; I did not go and see him for I had no gift or toy. I felt very sad for I had stood outside alone; he never wanted gifts if only I had known.

As an ever-glowing light began to shine quite strong, I searched my soul and I realized I was wrong. The child had grown quickly and his heart was strong, but true and he often told strangers the Father still loves you. I listened to him speak I watched him heal the weak. He never had any money yet he came from the land of milk and honey.

As an ever-glowing light began to grow and grow I watched the gentle man be put to death quite slow. He did not try to fight he did not swear revenge, he did die for my sins and now my soul is cleansed. This kind and gentle man that I thought I should fear is now my savior Jesus and in my heart I hold him near. He gave up everything so I may know him as king and now I worship him and his praises I do sing.

Amen

Faith in His Word

*Many question the word of The Bible they think that it is words
of just men
I believe it is the word of God true stories like Daniel and the
Lions' den
I don't need proof to know he is real I believe what I have
heard
I am a true believer in the Lord thy God for I have faith in his
word.*

*Making him prove himself is what many try to do
Just look around at nature and a sky made of blue
He's in the trees that blow and rain that falls and in every
living thing
Beautiful rainbows in the sky and sunsets made of gold are
what his colors bring.*

*The Lord is my master and it is his love that I will share
I carry it in my heart I take it with me everywhere
He has told us to love and honor him even if we look absurd
For I know I am going to heaven because I have faith in his
word.*

Charlotte Mae

Finding Jesus

When your life is filled with gloom and despair
And things get so ugly that even you don't care
Just look to the heavens and you will find
There's a giving spirit who's got you on his mind.

Hold out your hand and give him your heart
You will feel your soul heal right from the start
You'll begin to see life in a beautiful way
You'll enjoy waking up each and every day.

You now have found the friend who has saved your soul
His name is Jesus Christ and your heart is his goal
He will love you and protect you for to him you are great
He gave you that second chance in life when he sealed his fate.

How Do I Thank Thee?

For all you've given me Lord how do I thank thee?
You've shown me love and set my soul free
I'm often shamed by the way that I act
But you keep on loving me and that is a fact.
The cross was built so that I could be saved
My savior was killed so that my sins could be waved
I don't give praise as often as I should
But in me you always see nothing, but good.

How do I thank thee for giving me life?
You help to fill the world by giving a husband a wife
The blessings you give them are fruitful not small
You give them to many you give them to all
The love you have given is to be shared among two
It's man loving woman not the same like some others do.

I thank the Father from my heart
After all that's the best place to start
Your blessings are so many and your love is so good
It's hard to believe that you're still misunderstood
You're a powerful being and I hope the world can one-day see
That it is through your love that we can set our souls free.

Forgiveness

The heart is a very funny thing
You can fill it with evil or teach it to sing.
We are taught that forgiveness is the way
Yet, we forget to do it each and every day.
We store up inside all the hatred that we can
Then unleash it on others again and again.

Showing courtesy is what we all are missing
Letting others go before us is what I am wishing.
We see the skin not the person that's inside
And many people that are different have learned, it's
easier to run and hide.

We teach our children to look out for number one
We have forgotten to tell them that sharing too, can be fun.
It's a great big world of push and shove
And this world would be such a mess without God's love.

Most of us forget his teachings when he taught us to forgive
And if we all could do so this world would be a much better
place to live.

From Darkness to Light

As your eye's look to the sky you begin to wonder
What makes the lighting and sound of thunder?
When your darkness is upon you and all you see ahead is night
Trust in the goodness of the Savior to help you see his holy light.

They say believe none of what you hear and half of what you see
I say it only takes Jesus Christ to set your anxieties free.
There will be times when your soul feels lost
But remember for you Jesus paid the cost.

From darkness to light he changed all our fate
Now we are the lucky ones to meet him at the pearly gate
His hands reaching out and his heart filled with love
In God's beautiful kingdom in a wondrous world up above.

Charlotte Mae

Gloom and Doom

You say that your life is filled with gloom
When you think where you're going you see nothing, but doom
Just look to the sky and search for a way
To get you through your unhappy miserable day.

You feel you're burdened because your finances are many
Just think of the people in their pockets isn't any
Share with them, their needs are so great
Give them what you can it isn't too late.

Yes, we all see gloom and doom, just ahead of us some days
We look to make ourselves happier in many different ways
We forget that Jesus Christ is gracious and so giving
He helps you to be happy and want to go on living.

Amen

But You Loved Me

When times were hard and friends were few
I was so confused and did not know what to do
I looked to the bottle and thought I saw hope
I drank until I finally was at the end of my rope
Some saw me as a waste; I drank until I felt free
I thought no one cared, but you loved me.

When the bottle was empty and so was my soul
Making me whole again became your goal
Filling my heart with a love that was pure
And living a good life is what I would endure
Complete and whole is what I wanted to be
I thought no one cared, but you loved me.

Getting high was now in the past
And living for God became such a blast
I was alive and life had so much to give
I finally found a reason to live
As I sang your praises I finally did see
I thought no one cared, but you loved me.

God's Door is Open

When doors close in your face and you feel like you're losing the race; God's door is open. Sometimes friends are hard to find and you've got so much on your mind; God's door is open. You may not understand why you've been dealt the worst hand, but remember God's door is open.

When darkness surrounds your room and you're waiting for happiness to bloom; God's door is open. When the hands of time keep passing you by and you feel so old that you just want to cry remember God's door is open. We all have felt alone and where we would find comfort was unknown; God's door is open.

When life no longer seems worth living and you find people are no longer giving God's door is open. The future may change and life becomes strange, but with rainbows in sight and heaven shining bright, God's door will be open.

Going for the Gold

When you run with the human race you sometimes come in first place, you think you've won the gold, but soon you realize you're just another year old. You try and beat everyone at their own game, you think it will make everyone remember your name, but the name that remains on my lips is the one and only that holds the world in his grips.

I have a friend who competes with only one and good wins over evil when the day is done. He wins the gold that comes from my heart; he stays in first place right from the start. The Lord our savior will be your best bet, he will help you win that gold medal and your love he'll never forget, he smiles on you at every step you take your heart and soul he will never forsake.

Going for the gold can be hard to do, but with Jesus by your side he will see you through. With heaven's light shining down on me and the eyes of Jesus helping me to see, I know I can beat the race of evil and sin and God's kingdom will be my reward when I win.

Charlotte Mae

God's Love

G OOD AND PURE

O PEN IS HIS HEART

D OVES FREE TO SORE

S AVING SO NONE WILL PART

L OVING FROM WITHIN

O PENING OF ONE'S MIND

V OYAGE AWAY FROM SIN

E TERNITY IS WHAT YOU FIND

Goodbye My Wife

As I look up from my hospital bed, I see the eyes of the woman I have wed, her tears are many and her face so sad I wish that I could tell her that it's really not that bad. I love her so for she is my wife she's my soul mate, my partner, and she's been my whole life. I want to tell her to be strong; my Lord has promised I'll see him soon he says it won't be long.

As I look up from my hospital bed, I see an Angel shining bright he tells me I'm going home and it just might be tonight. He tells me of a land so great with streams and mountains just beyond the gate, he helps as the pain gets worse and from the Bible he quotes a beautiful verse. I see the lion with the lamb, it's such a pretty sight I know that I have won the battle and no longer need to fight.

As I look down from God's great kingdom, I see my friend's all weep I know they don't understand, but God's promise he did keep. I'm in a land that's filled with love and peace beyond compare no longer will I have to suffer there is no pain to bare. So cry no longer and hurt no more, my God has brought me home in beauty and splendor beyond belief forever I can roam.

Charlotte Mae

Grateful

As I watch my children sleep my heart becomes so very full
They are to me like a priceless and precious jewel
Two gifts from God to raise and teach them of his word
I believe that children should be seen and always should be heard
It is in remembering that they too are God's children and he is their father first;
Yet, some forget this and they only see their parents worst!

As I sit back and look at my life I see the pot of gold
The lessons I have learned suddenly begin to unfold
I have reached for the stars, but pulled down an empty hand
It wasn't until I surrendered my soul that life became so grand
We are confused in our thinking as we allow money to be our main need
This way of living only leads to emptiness, sorrow, and greed.

As I look to the future I am unsure of what road to travel
But praying for wisdom and truth my quest begins to unravel
I have given my heart to the one that died for me
He was put into chains so that I may be set free
I am so very grateful to God, for he is so good and kind
I love him truly with all my heart, my soul, and my mind.

Hands

His hands were soft and touched many sweet
His words were kind and made one feel complete.
He offered peace and fought for the right
Yet they stole him away like a thief in the night.

His hands were strong and held the weak
His voice would calm whenever he did speak.
He led many to the Father and God he was proud
When he ascended up to Heaven, the angels sang out loud.

His hands were hurt and scared from sin
Without that pain a new life could not begin.
He paid the price so my soul can be free
I can't believe such a love was given to me.

31

Charlotte Mae

He Came

He came a child of innocence to wear my sin
It was on the cross the pain was to begin
I never knew a man that never hurt any
Yet he paid the price for me and so many
His will was a strong one and to God he stayed true
He kept praying for others and his fate he already knew

He came in peace and loved the wicked and the good
The plan of the Father he knew and understood
He blessed all he met and the sick he did heal
Love for the world is what he did feel
He was gentle and kind and his friendship was true
Believe in him and the Father was all you had to do

He came in love and for this he did pay
But he arose like he said he would on that faithful day
He offered his blood so that many can live on
He gives us hope with each and every new dawn
His name is Jesus Christ and he is the savior of all mankind
Love him and peace in your heart is what you will find.

Amen

He came He died He lives

He came as a man of kindness true to his God and perfect in every way
As a human he was filled with love and he passed it along with each new day
His hands were strong, but would soon be scared; his face was sweet and kind
The sun would set on that faithful day when he would finally leave sin behind
He was the one that paid the price so that we would receive penitence
Each day he reminded us that he was the Savior he told us in each and every sentence.

He died like a man of honor with eyes that were filled with pain
The night came very quickly and soon the sky filled with rain
Many onlookers still did not see that he was more than just a man
But one that was dying too spoke, save me; softly he said yes I can
As the wind did blow and the believers did cry sadness filled the air
Before he died, he looked to the crowd and told how he would save them from despair.
He lives in the heaven by God's right hand and proud his father is too
Eternal life is what he gives and believing is all you have to do
The angels sing songs of delight and they praise him and he smiles
He is the one that paved the way and helps us with our tribulations and our trials
Life is complete because he loved us before the beginning of time
He is great in every way and I'm so thankful that as a Savior I can say that he is mine.

33

Charlotte Mae

He is All

Give to him your dreams to make real
He is the Prince of Peace and knows just how you feel.
He sees within your heart and can tell if it is true
He gave up his blood on the Cross to give life to me and you.

Dance and sing and rejoice in his name
His love is everlasting like an eternal flame.
He watches over us and keeps us safe from harms
When we enter into Heaven, he is waiting with open arms.

He is the sun and moon and the stars up above
His gift is a simple one, his life, and his love
He is the way to a kingdom that I know will never fall
He is my Savior Jesus Christ he is in every way my all.

He Is!

There are those who believe that God should prove his love
They are the same that think to get somewhere they have to push and shove
It is in faith you will find the ultimate truth
And it is my belief in the Father that keeps me in my youth.

Some say seeing is believing, but I say not
I am thankful each day and for everything that I have got
Questioning the lord is like defying his word
In the glory of the Heavens is where his voice can be heard.

Looking for signs will get you no where
God offers a love beyond compare
Just close your eyes and accept him into your heart
Trust in your feelings and know he'll never part.

He Will Hear

Ask for and he will hear, in your time of darkness there will be nothing to fear. He sees you as a child in need, on the cross for you he truly did bleed. His faith in you cannot be measured, his love for you he always has treasured.

Ask for peace and he will hear and when you're sad he will always be near. You cannot hide for he sees all; he picks you up whenever you fall. You are the light that shines through his eyes; you are the tears that fall whenever he cries.

Ask for forgiveness and he will hear he is always willing to lend a listening ear. He died on the cross so that you can have life the pain he endured cut like a knife. He's waiting in heaven with arms open wide; he loves us so much that's the reason that he died.

He Will Hold Your Hand

He will hold your hand when your fears are real
He is the one who truly knows exactly how you feel
He seeks out the poor and gives them riches of truth
To him we are all his children and we're still in our youth.

He will hold your hand in times of grief
It is through your faith you will feel relief
He offers a love that is good and pure
Your sadness and despair is what he will endure.

He will hold your hand when it is time to leave
You will witness your loved ones as they slowly grieve
But remember God's promise and his kingdom up above
Eternity will be filled with peace completeness and love.

Charlotte Mae

Heart of Gold

A heart of gold is what you'll find, a friend whose special trust worthy and kind. By your side he will stay when life seems it's worst, he will never let you down and with him you will always come first.

A heart of gold and a love that is true, he gave us the greatest gift; his life for me and you. His hands reach out for you to touch, we offer so little, and he offers so much.

A heart of gold and a life ever after, he touches our souls and our lives fill with laughter, he helps us to see that his love is the way we need to praise him and give thanks for our gifts each and every day.

Heaven

With gates made of pearl and streets made of gold, there are enough mansions for the young and the old. It is a place where the sun always shines bright and darkness never comes to cover God's holy light. It is a land made of beauty and fields made of green, there is only good and love no one is ever mean.

It is a place made of flowers and waterfalls of blue, each day is ever giving, and each moment feels brand new. With animals so kind and gentle that walk with each other side by side, never are they in danger never do they need to run hide.

Heaven is a place that God has made for me, it is a land of peace and beauty and a place where I am free. The lion with the lamb, the eagle with the dove, it is the land of milk and honey; it is a land that is filled with love.

Charlotte Mae

Hello My Lord

Hello my Lord how are you today
Thank you for everything is what I want to say
Your gifts are so wonderful and your love undying
I am not the Christian you want me to be, but truly I am trying

Hello my Lord your blessings are so great
Each day I awake is one more thing to appreciate
With land so green and skies so blue
To receive your gifts and to love you is all I have to do

Hello my Lord it is now time to sleep
You fill my soul with passion and it runs so deep
I give thanks for so much, but mostly for this day
A new one I will live to enjoy bless me with tomorrow I pray.

His Love is Always There

In a world filled with promises that are easily spoken
It's a shame how so many feel nothing when they are broken
Words come so freely a good heart to find is rare
I have a gracious and giving Savior and his love is always
there.

Too often we worship the famous and forget the true at heart
It is in our hunger to succeed that our selfishness can start
We reach out for that golden ring and find life is unfair
But if you will trust in Jesus Christ you'll see his love is always
there.

With child like eyes we only see the good
It is from evil intent that life becomes misunderstood
I have a friend and his gifts go beyond compare
He is the son of man and his love is always there.

Life is a gift we often forget to treasure
Heaven is a dream one cannot begin to measure
With Jesus in your life forever he will care
His promise will never be broken and his love will always be
there.

41

Charlotte Mae

His Pain

The day was dark and the clouds did cover the sun
As the fate for the gentle King of the Jews finally had begun
He prayed to his Father, while priests judged him on words that he spoke
They looked down on him, as if he were trash, but his spirit, it was not broke.

One lash of the whip and his skin broke and bleed
While a crown of thorns dug deep in his head
Tears filled his eyes and from the pain he cried out
Still…he stayed true, as he looked into the faces filled with doubt.

Soon arms that embraced the sinner, were now stretched out on a cross
His friends thought to themselves, "He's so kind, this is such a loss."
Sadly his body and skin were torn and his blood was shed for thee
It is through his spirit of giving that now allows our souls to be set free.

HOLIDAY'S

AS THE HOLIDAY'S APPROACH, LET'S NOT FORGET OUR LORD.
WE ACT LIKE SHOPPING IS A BOTHER AND IT MAKES US
FEEL SO BOARD.
WE FORGET TO HONOR OUR SAVIOR AND GIVE HIM ALL
THE PRAISE
WE'RE OFTEN BUSY RUSHING AND WALKING AROUND IN
A HOLIDAY HAZE.

WITH SNOWMEN IN THE WINDOWS AND SANTA AT THE
MALL
WE FORGET TO REMEMBER THE BABY THAT SAVED US
WHEN HE WAS VERY SMALL.
WE WISH EACH OTHER MERRY AND WE BUY SO MANY GIFTS
WE THINK THAT SPENDING MONEY OUR SPIRITS SOME TIMES LIFTS.

A BABY IN A MANGER IS WHY WE CELEBRATE
WHEN I WELCOME HIM IN MY HEART I ALWAYS FEEL SO GREAT.
JESUS CAME TO SAVE US ALL FOR HIM WE HAVE THIS DAY
ENJOY YOURSELF AND GO BE MERRY, BUT FORGET NOT, TO PRAY.

Charlotte Mae

How Do I know?

How do I know that there's a God, do I look for signs or put him to a test?
I hear people say he is not real so I set out on my own little quest.
I looked at the sky and saw the blue; I looked at my life and knew just what to do.
I opened my heart and offered my soul, learning of his love had become my goal.
The peace was real and I felt so complete, I felt an easiness from my head to my feet.

How do I know he will love me true, where do I go just to find a clue?
I walked for a day and then fell on one knee and then suddenly with a breath I felt free.
I felt a warmth I had never known and it was at that point that my faith had finally grown.
The wind did blow and it sang a song, it told me of God's love and I knew I did belong.

How do I know my soul is saved, they say there's a book that will hold my name.
I sat in the night and I pondered this thought and I realized my soul couldn't be bought.
God made me a promise and I do believe, his son died for me and there's no need to grieve
I trust my Lord and take him at his word, through my heart is where his promises have been heard.

I Have a God

I have a God who is caring and strong
He listens with his heart and to him I belong
He offers his love and always hears me when I talk
He is by my side and guides me as I walk.

I have a God who I can depend on in need
Taking care of me is his wonderful deed
He opens his hands and lifts me up when I am low
He's an awesome God and I do love him so.

I have a God that gives blessings in so many ways
He protects me from evil all my living days
He's a God to many and with you I will share
His love for you is simply way beyond compare.

I Hear

I hear so many people speak the good Lord's name, they mangle it, abuse it, and make me fell such shame.
His name is a special one and in we must trust, but still they go and use it, believing to curse is simply a must.
I try to tell them never use the Lords name in vain, but my words go unheard and God's tears fall like the rain.

I hear so many people blame the Lord, they say that it's his fault, but usually it's those same people that think forgiveness can be bought.
They tell me that he could have stopped the evil that was done.
I tell them "He did not bring the evil" no, my God was not the one.
They speak of a day when the world will end and longer it will be. I dream of a day when freedom comes and our Lord will set us free.

I hear so many people forget to give God praise, they go about their business in and ungrateful selfish haze.
I try and live each day to help my fellow man, I know that God wants that part of his wonderful and special plan.
I often wonder why he is so very forgiving, but if were not for his love, we would not get to go on living.

I Will

In a world of push and shove
You ask…is there really love
You search for peace and a true friend
The search seems so long that it may never end

Life seems so cruel it's hard to understand
It can be less painful if someone is holding your hand
"Hurry up and wait" is the motto of the day
And when things are difficult we all look for an easier way

Who will lift you when you are low
Who will strengthen your very soul
Who will know exactly how you feel
Many times Jesus has said, "I will."

Charlotte Mae

In Faith I Found Trust

As I traveled on my journey I wasn't sure I would survive
I felt the airplane moving and prayed when it landed that I
would be alive
It shook and began to vibrate and soon the noise was quite loud
My children and my husband folded their hands and with
heads bowed
A prayer they were saying as their lips trembled in fear
We were all so sure that certain death was very near.

The other passengers soon were all unsure and scared
I had been afraid before, but to this nothing compared
The sky was dark as the lights on the wing began to fade
Soon everyone was still as the announcement was made
In the pilot's voice I could hear his grief and stress
But I asked my God "would we make it" and he said..."yes."

Within minutes of prayer I felt a peace come over me
I could feel my fears beginning to be set free
The ride now was smooth and the sweat left my palm
All of the others seemed to be very calm
I now know believing in God is a must
For it is in my faith that I also found trust.

Amen

In God I Trust

"Show me a sign" I have often asked not believing in the truth
I had no fear of what would be when I was in my youth
Looking to the sky, but not seeing what was real
I was so confused so often I didn't really know just how to feel
I wanted so much and most of it for selfish gain
I didn't see it then, but I caused my own grief and pain.

Looking, but not seeing is what most of us do
We never see the light until our lives are almost through
Living for today some think is words of advice
But living for God at least your not just throwing dice
Live fast and die young are words I do not live by
Being kind and serving the Lord is what I'd rather try.

In God I trust with all my heart and soul
Being in his Kingdom will be my only goal
Looking into the eyes of my Savior will be my greatest gift
And my soul from this evil into Heaven he will lift
*To say thank you dear Lord for giving me life and allowing me
to love*
*Will be my first order of business when I meet my God up
above.*

Charlotte Mae

It Was Christ

It was Christ that was sent as a lamb to be stained with our sin
Forgiveness comes easy if you will only let him in
He is kind and generous with a heart that is bigger than the sky
We are so special to him we are the apple of his eye
His hands are scarred, but strong enough to hold
He's the greatest man I've ever known his story never gets old.

It was Christ that first cherished mankind
He died so that none would be left behind
He spoke of goodness and loving one another
To him we truly are his sister and his brother
Around his head was a crown made of thorns of pain
Now he sits by God where his kingdom he does reign.

It was Christ who first taught...love the sinner, hate the sin
And if we all live this then forgiveness can begin
We all have shame that lives deep within our heart
If you trust in Jesus you will feel you healing begin to start
He is the gift that God has given so please don't let his death be
in vain
It is through his blood you soul will be cleansed like sparkling
holy rain.

Its Times Like These

Its times like this when prayer is needed we must hear the warning and God's word be heeded. So often life just passes by with a fleeting moment and a blink of an eye. Look up to the heavens and ask him to see you need him to touch you and help your sadness be set free. He knows you are weak and need him so much, he allows us to lean on him he will be your crutch.

Its times like this that seem so bleak it is in the father and son our strength we'll seek, to have a friend like the Lord above is to have a true unconditional love. He reaches out to give us a hand with him by your side on your feet you will always land. We see the worst, but hope for the best we give it to God and in his hands let it rest.

Its times like this when we all need our friends and God is so great his angels he descends, they watch over us and touch us in a way like only they can on that very faithful day. God is the shepherd and we his sheep he loves true and he loves us deep, in times of despair when all hope is lost just remember you have a place in heaven because Jesus paid the cost.

Charlotte Mae

JESUS

J OY AND PEACE ARE WHAT HE GIVES

E NDURING SIN AS HE LIVES

S URRENDER ALL YOUR PAIN

U NDERSTAND A FRIEND IS WHAT YOU GAIN

S IMPLY PUT, JESUS IS THE SAVIOR AND HIS DYING WAS ONE'S GREATEST FAVOR.

Joyful Tears

Joyful tears stream down his face
He gives his love to every race
In his heart he will judge you not
When he gives you his love he gives all he's got

Joyful tears, but his body filled with pain
Hanging from the cross while his blood did drain
The day was dark and the sky was black
They all laughed as he said he would be back

Joyful tears now fill my eyes
For it is Jesus that hears my cries
It is his love that gave me grace
And in God's heaven I will always have a place.

Just Suppose

Just suppose if life were a play and God controlled all we do and say.
No will we would have no choices to make; Jesus would not have died on the cross for all of our sake.
Sin as we know it would not exist, no name in God's book, no he would not need to keep a list.
We would not learn the bittersweet lessons of life and there would be no need for us to be husband and wife.

Just suppose if you couldn't make a choice and if it were the right one you wouldn't need to be happy and rejoice.
You would do and say whatever he willed you to do; your life would be without feeling all the years through.
He would choose your friends and the people you meet; your life would be filled with hallow and never be complete.

Just suppose if God were not so loving and pure, the pain of life we would all have to endure.
He gives us a choice and lets us do what we will, he allows us to know right from wrong and teaches us how to feel.
He forgives us for the ugliest of sin and forever you'll be in his heart, he will always let you in.

Life's One Guarantee

As a child you dream of wonders and pretend
You enjoy the day and wish that it never would end
You see your life in a wonderful way
Waiting for the morning so again you can play.

As a teen you begin to see life unfold
The middle age seem to be so very old
You think you're invincible and life will go on forever
Growing old to you will happen never.

As an adult your wishes are tucked away
Getting through life is harder with each new day
But remember God's love and life's one guarantee
You'll always have my son and you'll always have me.

Charlotte Mae

Listen

Listen with your heart and you will hear God say
I am here to protect you each and every day.
As my child I want for you only the best
And you're tired and weary it is in my arms I want you to rest.

Listen with your heart and you will hear God sing
He sounds like the birds, the wind, and the bells as they ring.
His tune is soft and his words are sweet
They make a harmony sound as soon as they meet.

Listen with your heart and you can hear God cry
His word and his love people still deny.
The decay we have caused in a world built from love
Has caused tears and sadness in heaven above.
Although he weeps in his heart he still knows
That many of us love him and it is in our actions that it shows.

Look to me

Look to me and give me your pain
I promise to keep your tears from falling like rain
I will hold you and protect you to the bitter end
I am your savior, your Lord, but above all your friend.

Look to me for all of your needs
I judge you not and praise your good deeds
I reward you for patience and love for each other
Peace you will find when you treat each other like a sister and
a brother.

Look to me to end all of your sorrow
I give you hope for a brand-new tomorrow
I offer a world filled with blessings so true
Its called heaven and it's waiting for you.

Charlotte Mae

Love From Above

There's a gentle love that comes from above
In a world where the eagle fly's with the dove.
It is given to all of us free from cost
If you keep in your heart, you'll never be lost.

Times when you're sad and seem all alone
There's a friend by your side just waiting to be known.
His love is pure and yours for the taking
A friend for all eternity is what you'll be making.

So if your heart is heavy and you've lost your willingness to try
Just look up to the Heavens, God's big blue sky.
There's a love for you and he's waiting there to give
All the special things in life that make it wonderful to live.

Love Lives

In a land of golden roadways and silver skies
Is a land where the truth of goodness and purity lies
Rainbows of splendor with colors towering over steams
A place that is seen only in your dreams.

Tranquil is what you feel and peace is what you will find
All your hurt and pain in this world will be left behind
Grass that is green and soft to the touch, a world you will love
to explore
As soon as you see this wonderful land, you will understand it's
allure.

Living all your dreams that you kept deep within is the reward
you will be given
In a land filled with beauty and wonder is where you'll be
living
Trust in the Father and know that everlasting life is what he
gives
Join him in his home called Heaven where he, Jesus , and love
lives.

Charlotte Mae

Love that is Strong

Love that is strong is love that lives on, it fill you with hope and helps you to cope. Love builds up your dreams and never rips them to seams; it gives you such pride and won't ever push you to the side.

Love that is strong is love from the heart; it helps you through the hard times and will never part. It lives in your soul and grows; it opens the door to a warm loving way.

Love that is strong is what god has to give; it's deep in our hearts where he wants it to live. He gives us each day to enjoy his sweet love, and then he gives us much more in Heaven above.

Masterpiece

With eyes of blue and hair soft brown and a smile so bright
He has a heart so golden that it shines and gives day to the
darkest night
God used soft stokes as he created his son so that he would be
pure
His blood was bright red and his pain more than any man
could endure.

Wearing a robe of white and carrying a cross of wood
His eyes filled with tears, but his heart filled with good
The sky was blue, but soon would become black
His deed he did and never took his word back.

He truly is God's greatest work of art
His love for you, never will it part
A wonder to all, a true Masterpiece
A blanket of love and the world's Golden Fleece.

Charlotte Mae

Mercy and Love

Mercy and love is so special and so hard to find
We look in our hearts, but so often we're blind
Forgiving those who have shamed us is so hard to do
And then it becomes a struggle of who hurt who
When it all is over love is what you have lost
It's a shame before it happens that we don't see the cost.

Mercy and love is what Jesus often taught
Goodness into each life is what he always brought
He said forgive the sinner, but hated the sin
If you want to be a Christian that's a good place to begin
Offer your love and show your heart is good
It is through the language of the Lord that all is understood.

Mercy and love is what Jesus gave on the cross
If you don't allow him in your heart you'll feel such a loss
He brings peace and hope to a life that is unsure
Completeness and fulfillness is what you will endure
A soul that is lost, oh what glory it will behold
A testimony of being saved will be yours that can be told.

Amen

Is He Real?

I have been asked is he real? I just smile and tell them how I feel. Jesus is my friend and he's there when I'm low, he always makes me happy, and that's all that I know. In my hour of sorrow when there seems to be no tomorrow, he shines that light and I know that everything is going to be all right. In times of sadness when no one seems to care, he always sends me a sign and lets me know that he is there.

I have been asked is he real? Just knowing that he is a part of my life gives me such a thrill. He's there in the morning whenever I rise and he's there in the evening when I close my eyes. He reaches out his hand whenever I fall; he makes me feel much bigger whenever I feel small. At times of need when all I feel is despair, he whispers in my ear, my child I really do care.

I have been asked is he real? I simply tell them that I thank him for every meal. He has given me a home and has filled it with love he's as gentle and pure as the white winged dove. He sends you happiness when you thought there would be none, if you want to get to heaven believe me he's the only one. You ask me if he's real, well I can tell you this he's the only way to find that spiritual bliss.

63

Charlotte Mae

My Dream of Heaven

As I close my eyes I can start to see, an ocean of beauty and a great big tree.

The grass is green and the sky is blue, as I run through the field I can feel the summer dew.

The animals are kind, gentle, and sweet, as I fall asleep they lay at my feet.

The breeze is soft and blows quite slow, I have no map, but I know where to go.

The mountains are high, but their peaks are kind, as you slowly climb them you're amazed at what you will find.

The Eagle is waiting and fly away he will not, he will allow you to pet him and he won't move from that spot.

The waters are calm and the falls bathe you soft, as you climb on the hill that extends like a loft.

The deserts are warm with the sand between your toes and the wind gives a hug as it gently and slowly blows.

No buildings up high, no five o'clock rush, just quiet and peaceful and a very soothing hush.

The Lord in his splendor as he shares his greatest gift your soul to be saved and never will it drift.

Gifts of Nature

As I watch the sun begin to rise
I see God's beauty and cannot believe my eyes
His colors of love slowly unfold
And each time I see this it never gets old

With each hour that passes I see more of his treasures
Seeing his mountains is one of my greatest pleasures
With seas of blue and canyons of stone
I am reminded of his love and know I am never alone

As the evening falls and the stars shine bright
I see more of his gifts in the sky of night
He shares his love in this splendor we call Earth
And if you will look at it through his eyes, you will truly see it's worth

Charlotte Mae

My Greatest Friend

Making a friend sometimes can be hard to do
It's so hard to judge if one's heart is true
Some smile and lie and your feelings don't mean much
But others are kind and giving and your heart they do touch
Like the willow tree they will learn how to bend
I know someone unique and he is my greatest friend.

We all seem to be in a rush, but all we do is hurry up and wait
We fear that if we are too slow somehow we will always be late
Time is something that seems to be one's greatest gift
And when you give it you will find that a spirit you can lift
Just being there and listening can help a heart to mend
Turn to the precious one, for he is my greatest friend.

Life is hard and sometimes sad, but you will make it through
Making friends with each passing day will make it all seem brand new
You just may find that empty soul that needed someone to care
Who felt that one more lonely day was more than they could bare
There is the kindness of a stranger that will be with you until life's end
He is Jesus Christ my Savior and is his my greatest friend.

My Savior

A man made of love with a soul kind and warm
He came to preach God's word and the people they did swarm.
His gentle heart he opened and soon they ripped it out
Crucify him he's a trader the people all did shout.
Give up he did not; he loved each of them still
He knew he had to die he knew it was God's will.

They whipped him till he bleed and no longer could feel pain
He knew his hurt and sorrow would be our greatest gain.
He looked at them with love and knew it was not through
Again he faced his accusers and knew just what to do.
They put him on the cross so he could bare our shame
The people still did not believe and cursed his holy name.

His love was still undying and stronger than before
It was at that moment my sin and shame he wore.
He came to teach us love and die so that we may live
An innocent soul and blood is what he had to give.
I love this gentle spirit for he did me such a favor
He is indeed my friend, my king; he truly is my savior.

Charlotte Mae

Jesus Speaks

"As I wonder among my Father's desert
I begin to understand his plan
Pain and death is what I will endure
And sin will no longer rule
My pain will touch the hearts of many
But others will never come to know my sacrifice
My hands that held the sick will now hold nails
And my feet that were anointed will drip with blood
The whip will cut my skin, but no tears will I cry
I will keep you in my heart and it is for you that I will die
After I have passed I will return and be seen
And my followers will live to tell my story
Believe in me for I am the truth of the Living God
His love and my life is what will deliver you from evil
In his Kingdom I will await for you my child
An eternity of peace will be yours forever."

Amen

My Wedding Day

As I dressed to meet my husband to be
I began to pray and got down on one knee
Dear Lord I said as I wondered would I be a good wife
Help me to be loving to my husband all of my life
I fixed my hair and painted on my face
Time was ticking as I saw my dress of lace
My nails were done, but my finger bare
A ring of gold forever is what I would wear
The music sounded and my vial was set
I knew God was there when our eyes finally met
I felt a feeling of peace and love
That only comes from our Lord up above
We said our vows and sealed then with a kiss
Dating and being alone I knew I would not miss
As the ceremony ended and tear rolled down my face
I knew that in life I had finally found my place.

Charlotte Mae

His Blood His Love

*As he arose on his final day he stopped long enough to say
"I give to you all of my heart and on this day God's promise
will start."
He carried a cross as his back almost broke, but on his words
he made sure not to choke
He told of a love that was true and strong, he told us that God's
Kingdom was where he did belong
As the nails were hammered deep into his wrist, he cried out as
his body began to wiggle and twist
His feet that were tired and sore from the walk, were now
bleeding badly, but still he did not talk
Tears filled his eyes as he looked to the crowd, "He's a trader,
he must die"
someone said out loud
Soon his tears no longer did fall, he was now like a King who
was standing proud and tall
He looked upon the people as he called out God's name and for
those that believed
they would never be the same
His pain and suffering was only just the start, the true gift of
forgiveness had to come from
deep within his heart
He gave of his blood so that no soul should be lost, he gave of
his love and his
life had to be the cost.*

No Expectations

*Most people that you meet offer friendship with only half a
heart*
*You think you've found a confidant and your inner secrets you
do start*
*It is that search to be accepted and to feel that we belong, but
in seeking*
such a need sometimes we all go a little bit wrong.
*In giving you should not expect, but most of ignore this and
that is the cause of neglect.*

*In loneliness we reach out to others longing for the gentleness
that we get from our mothers.*
*We enter a world of fake feelings and fake friends we look for
light in the tunnel but soon find it never ends.*
*It's hard to find a hand to hold and even harder to find a heart
that is made of truth and gold.*
*Using others is what some do best they say their friendship is
real, but then give it in jest.*

*No expectations is what true friendship is all about, you lean
on each other and you're always willing to help one another
out*
*Your heart is forgiving and it dances with love you see it as a
blessing from the good Lord up above.*
You grow with each other and share each other's pain
A partner in life is through this what you will gain.

Charlotte Mae

One God Real Love

There is only one God filled with real love
He is the spirit of time he is to me all things
His hands raise the dead and free the living
He is greatness he is the true Abba.
In a world filled with hate he still loves
He is peace and hope throughout life
He is all things to man and so much more
Deep in the heavens he holds a kingdom for all
We wonder what he looks like yet we know
To him we owe so much still he asks for nothing
He is a God of love a being of wonder
He is the one God filled with real love.

Please…Forgive My Anger

As I pray I find myself asking for selfish things
I demand all the joy that my wants and wishes brings
When I feel my prayers are left unanswered or forgotten
I sometimes act like a child that is spoiled rotten
I stomp my feet and cry tears of disappointment
And it is in my faith that I begin to feel un-fulfillment

My heart becomes empty and my mind is filled with doubt
Why I love the Lord I try and figure out
I feel he has abandoned me and knows not what I need
But it reality my anger is really my greed
My guilt begins to surface, as I become aware
That God is still with me and he really does care

I begin to ask for forgiveness as I feel like a fool
I gave Satan a chance and my heart he did rule
He tried to make me think that I was not good enough to bless
And that my life was truly in a great big mess
Please God, forgive my anger for you love is my reward
I know now I am blessed I am loved by you my Lord.

Charlotte Mae

Priceless Love

Priceless love is love that is true
It stays with you the whole day through
It makes your life and world seem bright
In darkness it's your greatest light

Priceless love is love that is strong
And in your heart you carry a song
It helps your heart feel so very full
And the world somehow doesn't seem so cruel

Priceless love is love that is great
Priceless love won't hesitate
It teaches you to be fulfilled
And a happy life you can begin to build

Real Love

What is real love? Is it when the eagle soars with the dove? Is it when you find a love that's true and you stand by their side no matter what they do? Is it when the needy have no shoes on their feet and you give them clothing and a good meal to eat?

What is real love? Is it when a heart is able to look past a color or is when we care just because we are sister and brother? Is it when your money is no longer why you care or is it when your money you lovingly want to share?

What is real love? If you think about it, it is all of the above. You give from your heart because it is what God has taught, you give unselfishly without a second thought.

Charlotte Mae

Rainbow

R emembering you forever

A dding to your burdens never

I n good times and in bad

N ever leaving you sad

B ringing peace into your heart

O ffering you a brand new start

W ith you always, God

Amen

Shine Jesus Shine

When the morning sun kisses the day of new
I see Jesus shine and a sky filled with blue
He is gentle and giving as he offers his love
He watches over me from his kingdom above.

My savior has offered me such a great gift
My soul and my sprits he always can lift
He helps to guide me and keep me from harm
When I enter God's kingdom, it will be on his arm.

Shine Jesus shine, for you are the holy one
You have been chosen for you are God's son
I will worship and honor all that you are
As I look to the heavens I will see you as the
brightest shining star.

Charlotte Mae

Stepping Into a Trap

Sometimes it feels like I'm stepping into a trap
I want to forget the day, but problems just fall into my lap.
I stay awake for I cannot sleep
I feel so empty all I can do is weep.
I say a prayer and I hope for a friend
I wait through the night for my broken heart to mend.
I rise to a new day and see the sun so bright
I'm OK through the morning, but then I must face the night.
I open a book to help relax my mind
I open the drawer and what do I find?
A picture of Jesus I forgot I had,
and as I looked into his eyes I didn't feel so bad
There are days when we all feel like we're stepping into a trap,
but if you look to the heavens you'll feel your helplessness
unwrap.   Jesus is the way to make it through those unhappy
times
he guides you with love, peace, and the soft sound of musical
chimes.

Strength in His Arms

When the world seems unkind and my fears are great
My Lord my God always carries my weight
He shows his goodness and all of his charms
I always find strength in his arms.

Sometimes this world offers nothing, but pain
It's at that point he washes me clean with his rain
He watches over me and I know I will come to no harms
I always find strength in his arms.

I thank thee dear Lord for the gifts you have given
I know you will bless me as long as I am living
It is in your goodness and kindness that you show me the way
And I will carry your light with me each and every day.

Charlotte Mae

Thank You

Thank you dear Lord for your gifts made from love
Two beautiful children and a husband sent from above.
It is through you that we may come to know
The treasures in life that will help us to grow.

Thank you dear father for the friends in my heart
Help me keep them close to me so never will we part
You teach us to love and for one another always to care
You show us it is your way to never be selfish and always to share.

Yes thank you dear Lord for loving me with all of my sin
Without dear Jesus, heaven would not let me in
Each day here on earth that you let me live to see
Is a gift in itself and you give it for

Thank You God

Thank you God for all that you do
Your grace is great and your love is true
You pick me up and help me stay strong
With you in Heaven is where I truly belong
Touching my heart so that I can love
Saving my place in your kingdom above.

Thank you God for friends that are good
They help me in life when it becomes misunderstood
I often think of them as angels sent by you
To keep me honest in everything that I do
They offer words that can lift me when I'm sad or I cry
I know they will be there for me until the day that I die.

Thank you God for my savior Jesus Christ
His was the greatest gift of all his blood his life his sacrifice
His strength is with me each and every day
When I am lost he always shows me the way
To him I can never repay all that he gave
Forever I am in debt for my soul he did save.

Charlotte Mae

The Awakening Love

I am in complete darkness and cannot find my way out
I begin to panic and then I scream and shout
Before too long I can in vision a light
The fear that I felt no is no longer in my sight.

A gentle voice speaks of trust and love
The sound seems to come from heaven above
I cannot see anyone, but I know that they are there
I feel a peacefulness and it seems to be everywhere

My name is Jesus and I have come to ease your pain
Saving your soul will be my only gain
You're a child of my Father and to him you are a gift
Your emptiness and heartache through my blood I can and will
lift.

The promise of God's love will never leave you low
I gave up my life because he loves you so
Reach out to him and embrace his holy love
He awaits his child in his kingdom up above.

The Gift of Love

The gift of love is a precious one, it is given too many, but taken from none, it comes from the heart, but only if it's real, in a word it can say exactly how you feel. You can search for this gift but find it not, it is given of free will, and it can't be bought.

The gift of love comes without any cost and as long as you have it you'll never be lost. You can give it to others and can show them the way; you'll find it deep in your heart it's there every day.

The gift of love is God's gift to you; he gives it to each one of us to keep our hearts true. His love can keep us from a life of despair as long as you take it with you everywhere.

Charlotte Mae

The Greatest Sin

The weight of sin is great...but we have been spared
It was because of Jesus and how much he really cared
He bore our sin and wore our shame
He blesses you each and every time you speak his gentle name

He was judged because he spoke the truth
It all began when he was a child and still was in his youth
He brought peace and hope and saved those that were lost
To enter Heaven is possible for his blood hath paid the cost

It's amazing to me so many today still have so much doubt
Just open your heart and let him in...the truth is not hard to
figure out
To close your heart and close your mind and not let the Son of
God in
Not to trust in Jesus Christ...to me is the all time greatest sin.

The Heart of Heaven

Some say he is the Lamb of God sent to bare our shame
He is kind and good and to him each face has a name
His eyes watch over us and protect us with each passing day
There is a place in Heaven for all, for Christ hath paved the
way.

He lives in a kingdom that is golden and waits for all who
believe
And when we are hurt and sad along with us he will grieve
His love is so wonderful and can fulfill one's soul
When he died on the cross saving mankind was his greatest
goal.

Jesus Christ is truly the Heart of Heaven and the Savior to all
He lifts you up and carries you whenever you fall
He sees you as a child, for to him you are everything
Getting you closer to God all mighty is what he is trying to
bring.

Charlotte Mae

The Lamb that Roared

There was a lamb born on a very special night
As soon as he grew up his purpose took its flight
He spoke of peace everywhere he walked
Words sounded like songs every time he talked
Offering his heart and sharing his love
Gentle and kind like a soft white dove
Riches and jewels was something he didn't need
His heart was very generous and knew no greed.

Thoughtfully he listened as many bent his ear
And when they were finished who he was became very clear
Feeding the hungry and healing the sick was what he did best
Bringing God's word to unbelievers quickly became his quest
As the sun set on the cross of sin, Jesus gave his life that day
When they removed it from the dirt his body there did lay
They said he would never rise from that cross-made of board
But how wrong they were, he became the Lamb that roared.

The Lion and The Lamb

In a peaceful land with skies of blue
Live two wonderful animals and to each other they are true
Fight they do not, both hearts are filled with love
They know that harmony is what their world is made of
Run freely with each other is what they do best
As they curl up with each other, it is time for them to rest.

As the lion watches over the lamb he is gentle in his ways
He makes sure to be careful in all the games he plays
They are strong as one and complement each other
The lion protects the lamb as if he were its mother
The lamb is kind and teaches the lion to care
Never are they alone they go together everywhere.

The lion and the lamb are gentle, but strong
To each others world is where they belong
They offer to each other an undying gift
Peace and strength that will never drift
In God's kingdom of love forever they will live
Friendship true and beautiful, forever they will give.

The Love of Money

The love of money can often rule, to those who worship it they sometimes act cruel. It turns a friend against another; it turns a sister against a brother. It makes you want material things in life and many times it is the cause of a husband to leave a wife.

The love of money can cause some to kill they take what they want and never do they feel. It makes us wish for more than we've got and often makes us act like something that we're not. It causes many to be very greedy they think about themselves and not of the needy.

The love of money is not what Jesus set out to preach; share with each other is what he tried to teach. It causes some to forget the Father's way; it's mine all mine is what their hearts will say. The love of money will someday make you broke; riches is in loving one another and that's what Jesus spoke.

The Prince of Peace

As a child he was wise and always very caring
He never hurt others and always believed in sharing.
As he grew he taught God's word and proved he was God's son
He told us to believe in the father and the holy one.

He told us of God's kingdom and spoke of a wonderful place
We enter into this world only by God's grace.
In sinners he saw good even when they were cast out
He was The Prince of Peace and that's what he was about.

He was put to death and committed no crime
God had to save the world he knew it was the time.
To this day his blood still pays the price of sin
It's only by his faithfulness that heaven will let us in.

Charlotte Mae

THE PROMISE

As I lay here on this cross I will remain faithful to you

I will love and forgive you no matter what you do

My blood is given so that yours can be spared

Sacrificing his son for you is how much the Father really cared

As I join the angels and take my place in God's kingdom above

I will write your name in Heaven's book of love

God's promise is done; my blood was shed for thee

When you reach the gates of Heaven the first one waiting there will be me.

The Saving Son

As God sat up in Heaven and gazed upon mankind
He thought "A true one will be very hard to find."
It was certain that blood must be shed for the price of sin
But finding a pure one was where he had to begin.
The day passed and soon fell into the night
He tried to find the right one; he tried with all his might.

The world became so much bigger and the sin was everywhere
It seemed that no one with a heart would ever show that they did care
The Angels in his Kingdom all said that they would go
But the lamb that he would send would be the only one that would know
My son come here to me I have something to say
You are the Lamb of God; yes your blood is the only way.

His son looked in his eyes as tears began to flow
"I understand my Father, now is my time to go."
"I am proud to be the one to save your children of the Earth."
"I will never let you down; I'll begin the day of my birth."
And so Jesus kept his promise, his blood did spill that day
Mankind can now be saved; his life was the only way.

Charlotte Mae

The Serpent

In a garden filled with wonder and beauty it was no surprise
Evil could not leave it alone so he filled the woman with lies
With a long and slimy body he moved and found his prey
And now he crawls upon his belly even now until this day

He thought he was unstoppable that evil could beat good
But when God showed his anger his fate he understood
Smart he thought he was when Eve fell for his story
But truly God would be the victor and have the only glory

So man did show his weakness and still continues today
But the serpent was the loser and now he's lost his way
The garden now is clean and free for God to roam
It's now a part of Heaven a place that God calls home.

The Ultimate Celebrity

A celebrity is someone so fine
It is in the limelight that they will shine
I know of one that seeks no fortune or fame
He's the ultimate celebrity and God is his name

Celebrities are sometimes cruel and quite vain
And with their actions and words they can cause such pain
But the ultimate celebrity will never leave you low
It is in his presence that you'll feel your heart and life grow

Yes, celebrities can hurt you and sometimes make you cry
They make empty promises and you know their words were just
a big lie
But the ultimate celebrity our Lord our God above
His promise is simply this…"I will always give you love."

Charlotte Mae

The Wonder

The true power of God is a wonder to me
He blesses us so wonderfully and helps our soul be free
His word is true and his love is strong
If you walk in his light you'll never go wrong

He is generous in his giving and fruitful in his love
When his son gave up his precious life it was you he was thinking of
Each sunrise is a new day the he offers you to share
Each sunset is a splendor with beauty beyond compare

Trust in the Lord and give him your all
Never will he hurt you, or allow you to fall
His kingdom has been built for an eternity of love
His compassion is all around you and it fits like a glove.

Time to Believe

I have always believed that seeing is believing, but not now
I am different these days God's love has shown me how
I had lost my way in a world filled with pain
But I knew it was time to believe and now it's my greatest gain.

They say if you can't touch it that it's not real
I trust my heart for it tells me how I feel
I now have faith and my problems no longer make me grieve
I have given God my soul it is finally time to believe.

The art of love is simply trusting in the King
With a tune in my heart his praises I softly sing
It is the weight of my sin he will gently relieve
I am now reborn because I took the time to believe.

Charlotte Mae

To Each a Gift is Given

To each a gift is given each time the sunrises and night falls
Mother Nature in her splendor is what God gave to share
His love is all around us and often is taken for granted
With forgiveness that is unmeasurable we often feed on it
He offers us eternal life if only you will believe
So many question his existence why can't they see
He is in the birds that sing and the beauty of the ocean
The rain that falls and the wind that blows
His music is in the trees as they sway and the thunder as it
roars
He lights up the sky with bolts that are bright
He is an awesome God that should be loved and worshiped
He demands respect, but at the same time earns it
He is the Lord thy God and he is mighty
He is the keeper of my soul and in him I trust.

To Know Him is To Love Him

As the sun set on that faithful day the sky was filled with rain
Those that believed in the Savior felt only anger and pain
They did not understand that his soul was who he was
And all across the land his death was now the buzz
His body was wrapped and hidden behind a wall of stone
But still the talk went on in death he was not left alone
They said he was just a man and yet they feared him so
It's a shame the real Jesus so many would never know
Still some stayed true and trusted in his love and in his word
His soft and gentle voice again to them was heard
They knew he was the profit they knew him deep inside
And they knew he had forgiven the ones who had denied
He blessed his followers and told them to go and teach
The sinners of all lands were whom they tried to reach
They told about his story and how his life was not so grim
And each man ended by saying,
"To know him is to love him."

Charlotte Mae

Today

Today is what scholars say is the birth of my Savior
It's so hard to believe with everyone's behavior
They rush around and spend money that will leave then in debt
And when they receive their credit card bill the feel nothing,
but regret
It's sad that this day has become one where gifts only come
from the store
And the true meaning of Today so many will ignore.

The wind and the birds all sing a precious song
For they know the truth and what we humans are doing wrong
The stars are bright and the mountains bow down to the King
The bells in the churches on the day all too will ring
The angels up in heaven celebrate this wonderful birth
But why we honor this day is forgotten here on Earth.

Today I will ask my God to forgive me for being blind
For when Jesus comes I do not wish to be left behind
I will remember on this day that a precious baby was born
And how on his final day his body from the cross was torn
I will honor and worship him today all of the days that I live
And as a gift on this special day to him my soul I give.

True Love That Comes From Above

You may wonder where to find love
And you ask yourself what you are made of
Looking for answers, but finding none
Thinking that you are the only lonely one

Looking for true love many find pain
They feel such a loss that finding love would be such a gain
They need only to open their heart and look to the one
The Father, the Spirit and the Holy Son

True love is love that comes from above
It soars through your life like a gentle dove
Freeing you from sin and pain that can break your heart
Trusting in Jesus Christ is a wonderful start.

Charlotte Mae

Truth in Every Word

Softly his lips move to utter words of hope
In those words we find in darkness we can cope
He speaks of a Father that none can see or feel
But if you open up your heart you will know he is real
I truly believe what I have heard
For there is truth in every word

I have read the stories that come from the book his Father
wrote
I hear his praises when he sings they are in every note
His body stays still as he describes his Father's land
As he talks of a Kingdom beautiful and grand
Some say his stories are false and absurd
But I believe there is truth in every word

As the years go by his lessons we must not forget
His songs are sang with each and every sunset
His soft words are heard in the wind as it blows
And with each passing generation his story still grows
Remember when he spoke it was clearly; not slurred
Forever more there will be truth in every word.

View of Love

This is a view of what love is all about
You speak softly to others never needing to scream and shout.
Teaching only good and showing how you feel
Knowing love is right and knowing it is real

This is a view of how love can be given
Reaching out to each other especially while we are living
Showing that you care and offering words of hope
Helping when we're down and in times when it's hard to cope.

This is a view of how love can be shared
Opening of one's arms and showing that you have always cared
Forgiving the hurt and the pain that has broken your heart
Living more like Jesus Christ in a world, that can tear your soul apart.

Charlotte Mae

Who Was He?

A babe was born in the dark of night
Three wise men were guided by a star lit bright
Silent he was and cry he did not
Each eye did stare, as he lay in one spot
His body was small, but his heart was great
He was the Son of God who became Jewish bait.

The years did pass and he was kind and good
His preaching to some was misunderstood
He lived God's way and tried to teach others
His love was given freely to his sisters and his brothers
With arms strong he held many that were weak
He said what he wanted and didn't even have to speak.

As he was put on the cross many laughed, but some cried
They realized who he was as soon as he died
The sky grew black and the angels did cry
Who was he a child asked and why did he die
A soul that was giving with a love that is pure
. He suffered for the sin of mankind...death is what he had to
endure.

Why Me?

When things get too rough and you just can't give enough you ask why me?

When money is shy and there's nothing you can buy you ask why me?

When your car breaks down and you're on the other side of town you ask why me?

When love is hard to find and others are so unkind you ask why me?

When others seem to be lucky in riches and you're out digging ditches you asks why me?

When you go before God and he tells you how much he loves you, you ask why me?

He answers; my child you were loyal and giving and now in heaven is where you will be.

Charlotte Mae

He Is Divine

*Of all the stories of the past there is only one that will truly last
It is a story of a boy who grew to be King and still till this day
his praises people sing
He was kind and good and never turned a heart away and he
still gives his love even till this day
He befriended each and every soul that he met and once you
looked upon his face his beauty you were never able to forget*

*He dressed in rags and lived among the poor and all the
treasures of life every day he would explore
He blessed the children as he told the stories of great and when
they asked him about his Father never did he hesitate
He told them of a God that was strong, but good and to his
surprise most of them understood
He described a Kingdom with streets paved in gold and each
time he spoke of it his story never grew old*

*Then came the day that silence replaced his soft and silky voice
he did what he had to do for him there was no choice
Accepting his fate in the name of God's love he knew he'd
speak again in the Heavens above
He is the Prince of Peace for to me he is devine he is the Savior
of the soul and I'm glad to know that he is mine.*

With Open Eyes

Have I been so blind that I cannot see his love
He watches over me, as does the Father up above
I am undeserving of all his gifts and praise
And yet he keeps on giving as the sun makes it's new days
I welcome him into my life and it comes as no surprise
My heart sees clearly now with open eyes.

As I wake my Savior blesses me and puts a song in my heart
It is then that I allow my day to begin with a new start
Putting anger aside as he would want me to do
I ask him for patience the whole day through
I listen to his words for he is very wise
I understand him fully now with open eyes.

He asks so little and gives so much
He heals the sick with a single touch
My love for him is deep and strong
With Jesus in my life I can't go wrong
I wear my love for him proud with no disguise
I give him my soul lovingly with open eyes.

Words of Love

A gentle man who was kind and good, when I was sad he understood.
He made me laugh when I was down; he made a smile out of a frown.
With words of wisdom he taught me much; when I needed a hug, he had just the right touch. A smile so bright the room did shine I'm so very proud that his love was mine.

With hands so strong mine they did hold; his heart was weak, but it was made of gold.
A Fishermen in the sea of life, a loving husband to his wonderful wife.
A friend to many when they had none; when you needed someone to listen, he was always the one.
A grandfather who always was there and his heart showed that he really did care.

A Christian to the bitter end, in Jesus Christ he always had a friend.
A man so special in every sense of the word, his prayers to be in God's kingdom where finally heard.
A loving man who gave so much and complained about it never It is deep in my heart that he will now live forever.

Amen

Y 2 K

They spoke and said that the end was near
The world would end and everyone was living in fear
Get water and food and soon it became a race
But I stayed cool and believed in God's grace.

The media cried and claimed that missiles might fly
The next day their rumors they would try to deny
Forts were built and some hid away for the night
The next morning God was still there with his sun shining bright.

Y2K was just hype now we see
Man is still living and the birds flying free
You just have to trust in God and know that he takes his time
And why he does should be no reason or rhyme.

The Meek

There is a saying that only the strong survive, but the Bible says that the meek shall inherit the earth. I believe that God has a plan for us all and he puts it into motion right from birth. In this day and age kindness is viewed as a weakness and people treat you as if you are small, but God sees it differently; to him they are great and he puts them above all. In a world of push and shove the meek are seen as dumb and slow, but in the world of Heaven their time on Earth is time for them to grow.

A heart that is good is something to be treasured, but in a world filled with evil it's our wealth on how we are measured. Being rich with worldly goods is how others see you as being great, but it is up in Heaven that lays our true and holy fate. Giving gifts made of gold can make one quite the king, but I believe that love is what God wants us to bring. The world sees you as poor when you haven't money to throw around, but it is in God's kingdom where your fortune will be found.

We all can learn from those who are giving and caring, it is God's message above all that they are sharing. He speaks to them and opens their heart it is in loving them that God wants us to start. Loving and caring for one another is what the meek seem to do the best, and until they have pleased the Lord they cannot seem to rest. They are good, they are strong, they are the meek, but one thing they are not and that is weak.

ABOUT THE AUTHOR

As a Christian I felt it very important to tell the world how much I truly love God and His son Jesus Christ. At the same time I wanted to give something back to God. As he put pen and paper in my hands he told me to unite his words. Two years later I completed His book, *Amen*. This is His work, not mine… I was just blessed enough to get to write it.

All profits from this book will be used to do His work. They will help to feed the hungry, heal the sick, clothe the naked, and spread His word. In buying this book you will help to do God's work and he will be pleased.